PRACTICING
THE
PRESENCE

HAZELDEN

Hazelden Educational Materials
Center City, Minnesota 55012-0176

ISBN: 0-89486-858-6

Editor's note:
Hazelden Educational Materials offers a variety of
information on chemical dependency and related
areas. Our publications do not necessarily repre-
sent Hazelden's programs, nor do they officially
speak for any Twelve Step organization.

*That deep emotional conviction of the
presence of a superior reasoning power,
which is revealed in the incomprehensible
universe, forms my idea of God.*
　　　　　　　　　　—Albert Einstein

There isn't only one correct idea of God. For some of us, God is manifest in nature—in the forests and flowers and waterfalls. Others may see God in people's faces—the wisdom and endurance of the very old; the innocence and wonder in the very young. The mystery of the planets and their orderly rotation around the sun, that the sun rises and sets without fail, provide for many of us awesome reminders that some*one* or some*thing* is in charge.

The beauty of these concepts is that they are all true. God is big enough to encompass what any of us conceive God to be. It's not important to have an exact understanding of God; it's only important to believe. With belief we can begin to know freedom from worry, and have the courage to take whatever actions are right for us now.

———————————

Permission for our own belief in God is one of the gifts of our Twelve Step program. Today will flow with ease if I let the God of my understanding in.

God is in charge.
　　　—Daily Word, *November 10, 1987*

A basic truth in our life, about which we need never be concerned, is that we are in the care of a loving God—always. And we can feel and unquestioningly know this presence if we choose to acknowledge it. When we take a moment to reflect on our past good fortunes—that we found this program, that our relationships with others are on the mend, that we harbor deep-seated fear far less often—we can use them to bolster our faith that our Higher Power is here, now, and will remain our constant, caring companion.

For some of us, faith in a greater Power comes easily. But many of us begin to have faith only through Acting As If. By quieting our mind, visualizing a loving presence, and breathing in the warmth and comfort, we can find the peace that *is* God. Through "practicing the presence," we'll strengthen our faith and ensure our peacefulness.

———————————

I can feel the peace I desire today through my own efforts to remember God.

The more I want to get something done,
the less I call it work.

—Richard Bach

A change of attitude can transform any arduous task from something dreadful to something filled with opportunity. We can play a part in how we encounter the moments in our life—we don't have to be victims. When we're involved, rather than passive and detached, we open ourselves to the possibility for greater joy and a fuller understanding of life.

A small yet profound change of mind-set allows us to see a seemingly mundane task, like raking leaves, as a chance to experience God's presence and acknowledge nature's mysteries, rather than just another bout with dirt, boredom, and blisters. It's possible to see the miracle of life and experience the joy of living in any activity.

We are alive—here and now—so that our purpose in life may continue to be fulfilled; whatever lies ahead today can be a further revelation of that purpose.

————————————

I will enjoy the opportunities to fulfill my purpose in life today.

It is what we all do with our hearts that affects others most deeply.
— *Gerald Jampolsky*

If we vigilantly let our heart determine how we are to respond to every situation or experience in our life and to every person with whom we're sharing our journey, our path will be less bumpy. We have the opportunity every moment to ensure a smooth trip today. By choosing to see and speak from our heart, we'll find peace. We'll be offering the gift of peace to others too.

Our heart is the home of our Higher Power whose wish for us is peace, joy, and a constant state of inner well-being. These gifts are ours to experience through the act of sharing our peace, joy, and love with others.

We never need to *long* for security, stability, or better outcomes in our life. We can learn how these gifts are contained in our own actions.

———————————

I desire peace and joy in my life today and I will feel it every moment that I listen and act from my heart.

Discipline is the basis of a satisfying life.
—Katharine Hepburn

When trying to reach a goal, we may tire of the constant effort that is required of us, or we may rebel against the structure that's necessary to keep us focused. We often long for what we remember as a freer, more spontaneous time in the past.

It's helpful to remember that our goals come from our desire for change. We can see each yearning as God's invitation for us to move in a new direction. And we can be sure that we have God as our helpmate throughout the journey wherever our destination may be.

Goals that inspire us to act bring meaning to our life. We make progress in moving toward them, and our feeling of satisfaction and renewed sense of purpose will motivate us to persevere to their completion.

The comfort of regular conscious contact with our Higher Power, as we seek always to align our goals with God's will for us, will carry us to the fulfillment of our goals.

———————

I will seek direction and strength from God while moving toward my goals today.

Because you cannot see him, God is everywhere.
                    —*Yasunari Kawabata*

What a nice reminder that God is everywhere, even when we don't remember God. Many of us still spend time each day trying to manipulate future outcomes and trying to control other people in the process. We wear ourselves out trying to control the uncontrollable, while God patiently waits to receive our burdens. All we need to do is hand them over: God's presence is here, now.

When we surrender all our concerns to God— both our failures and successes—we begin to realize the breadth of God's care and the constancy of God's presence in our life. We have always been close to God, as close as our breath.

Learning to acknowledge God as our protector and guide is exhilarating and eases our every step, thought, plan, and dream. We are learning that we can do nothing alone, but we can do anything if we just let God join us in partnership.

I have God as my companion always. I'll remember that today and be at ease.

*A little lifting of the heart suffices; a little
remembrance of God, one act of inward
worship are prayers which, however
short, are nevertheless acceptable to God.*
—Brother Lawrence

Our days are filled with busyness. Few of us
seem to have time to pause for a breath of fresh air,
let alone take time out to commune with our
Higher Power. But if we practice knowing that God
is present in our life, and keep at it until it becomes
habitual, we find ourselves noticing that we are not
alone.

And it doesn't take much to establish a connection. Just thinking that God cares is enough
to do it. Realizing that we can commune with
God through other people does it too. A smile, a
sympathetic word, a pat on the back, and we are
connected.

---

*I will practice sensing God in all that I do and in
everyone I meet.*

The answer to personality problems is found in a quiet return to Godlike thinking.

—Science of Mind
magazine

When we're edgy and critical or perhaps feeling inadequate or depressed, we've lost our attunement with God. And when acting the way God would have us act is no longer our priority, our character defects once again emerge and, in time, grow ever more numerous.

We can make the simple decision to always check out our proposed behavior against the behavior we know is from God. When we remember to think of God first before proceeding, we avoid unnecessary conflicts; we refrain from consciously hurting anyone; we manage to take our experiences restfully, moment by moment.

There's really no mystery to having a rewarding and peaceful life. Those we notice who do have likely made a more frequent companion of God than we. The decision to work more on our own friendship with God is an easy one to make.

─────────────

I will act according to God's wishes today and, in the process, strengthen our friendship.

It is not the image we create of God which proves God. It is the effort we make to create this image.
—Pierre Lecomte du Noüy

Not very many of us have the truly dramatic spiritual experience that dispells, for all time, our insecurity and our doubts about God's existence. We may know someone who has been this fortunate, but most of us have to give frequent or daily attention to prayer, meditation, and perhaps affirmations in order to develop the faith that can come to everyone.

Our path for developing conscious contact with God makes God a familiar companion in our daily life. Our thoughts of God can remind us that God cares and is in charge. Exercising our mind in this way is not unlike exercising our body. Just as our repeated physical efforts strengthen our muscles, our belief is strengthened into faith when we make the remembrance of God's presence a daily practice.

I will remember God today.

Whoever is happy will make others happy too. He who has courage and faith will never perish in misery.
—Anne Frank

Acknowledging our gratitude for the blessings in our life releases the happiness that we sometimes keep hidden within our heart. And happiness can be contagious. We all know people who are always bubbly, who always look on the bright side of events, who genuinely inspire happiness in us when we're around them. We, too, can serve as a catalyst for happiness in the lives of others.

Knowing that we're never left alone to solve any problem or handle any situation relieves us of much of the anxiety that crowds out happiness. Having God as a constant companion, and having faith that we are moving toward the best outcome for the present circumstance, makes happiness a far more frequent visitor in our life. Happiness becomes habitual when we keep our focus on God as our play's director, the source for all our decisions.

I will share happiness and my faith in God with others today.

*There is no area of personal challenge in
your life that God's love cannot solve.*
                                    —Mary Kupferle

We seem so certain at times that we alone must find the solution to a nagging, troubling situation. As we obsessively focus our attention on the problem, we feel even greater frustration when the solution eludes us.

Most of us have heard that we keep a problem a problem by giving our attention to it—by the power we give it. What we generally forget is that placing our focus on God instead, while believing in God's love for us and God's concern for our plight, will reveal the solution quite quickly.

God's love is constant. God's willingness to care for us, always, is there to be discovered. Our challenges offer us opportunities to remember God's presence. All challenges, though painful on occasion, are really our invitations to walk a stronger spiritual path.

———————————————

*God's love accompanies me everywhere today. I won't
stumble if I remember this.*

Conscience is, in most men, an anticipation of the opinions of others.
                              —Sir Henry Taylor

We are no longer in doubt about the right actions to take toward others. The program's Steps clarify what is appropriate behavior. Thus we know that doing any injury—physical or emotional—to other people harms us as well as them.

One of the many rewards of recovery is being free to live without guilt. Name-calling, harmful gossip, intentional put-downs, hateful rejections no longer provide the perverse pleasure of years gone by. We now recognize the subtle joy of sincere and loving efforts. We find this joy in calling a friend who is faced with a painful decision, picking up groceries for an elderly neighbor, extending our friendship to the new person at work. We no longer need the fear of what others will think to curb our spiteful actions.

Our conscience may still guide our actions at times, but as we grow in our recovery, we begin to intuitively know what keeps us on track and in sync with God.

I will follow my God-given intuition today.

We find that as we become more centered within the Higher Power part of us, our ego becomes less real, less threatening, less compelling.

—Jerry Hirshfield

It's a struggle at times for us to remember that our Higher Power never moves away. God is as close as our breath, awaiting our invitation to take charge. Frequently this strikes us as *new* information. But each time a friend or a particular reading triggers our recall, we relax, because we know that God is taking over. Once again we trust that all is well.

It's our ego that fights giving up control during the early stages of many of our troubling experiences. We are frustrated again and again as we try to force what we think is the best solution; again and again, in the end, after we've finally given up the struggle, God smooths the path.

This program guarantees us a smooth trip every step of the way. All we have to do is give up control to God who is always waiting for us to turn our attention from our problems to God's presence.

I will feel peace and joy throughout today because I'll remember my Higher Power's presence.

Never forget that God tests His real friends more severely than the lukewarm ones.

—Kathryn Hulme

All of us have experienced times when we felt forsaken, when we were no longer certain that a Higher Power really existed, was present within us, and in charge of our life. The unexplainable death of a friend or parent may have pushed us to our limit of belief. Or the painful end to a relationship we'd been sure was part of God's plan shook our faith.

We can't expect to be free of all strife in our life just because we walk a spiritual path. By simply being alive and in relationship with other people we will know pain as well as happiness.

As we open ourselves to a spiritual life, we discover a power greater than ourselves that sustains us. This power is available, even when we suffer beyond our understanding. And we can rely on this power that fills us with peace every time we turn over what we can't handle.

———————

Today I will turn over all my concerns to God.

Let God love you through others and let
God love others through you.
                                          —D. M. Street

Every person in our life is an invitation to know God better. We may understand this intellectually, but it's all too easy to become self-absorbed and distant. We see other people, but not with our spirit-filled eyes; we don't see them as emissaries of God who have been sent to teach us about love.

More frequently, when we first really notice the people around us, we compare ourselves to them, checking to see how we measure up physically or intellectually or even spiritually. Seldom does our first thought or action express unselfish love.

We may have to practice the act of loving for years before it comes naturally. But it *will* become an automatic reaction in time, just as self-loathing may have been the automatic reaction in years past.

We can reach God through the men and women sharing our journey. It's no accident that our path is filled with people: through them God intends for us to learn to love, and thus know God.

———————————

I'll rejoice in my many invitations to know God's love today.

Truth will correct all errors in our minds.
—A Course in Miracles

The profound inner truth of our life is that we have a lifelong partnership with God. As we strengthen our awareness of this constant, love-filled presence, we'll be less able to cloud our mind with critical thoughts. Any thought we choose to hold that is not blessing someone harms us as much as the other person. Returning our thoughts to God, even when our ego is struggling to think mean thoughts, will release us from the bondage of negativity.

Our Twelve Step program offers us freedom from this bondage every time we contemplate the Third Step. Letting God take charge of our will promises us freedom from harmful actions and thoughts. How lucky we are to have this guidance in our life. Our teachers are everywhere. From some of them we experience direct communication from our Higher Power. From others we gain countless opportunities to let our Higher Power direct our actions toward love.

I will correct my thinking today by filling my mind with the presence of God rather than unholy thoughts.

It is not true that suffering ennobles the character.

—W. Somerset Maugham

We've heard the phrase "No pain, no gain" many times. Perhaps we've also heard "Pain is inevitable. Suffering is optional." We may want to consider these carefully before assuming they are absolutes. It's far more sensible to believe that our attitude determines whether we find a situation painful. We can be overwhelmed by suffering if we choose. Or we can accept our changing circumstances as natural and growth enhancing.

If we stay centered on God throughout change and let this relationship comfort and quiet us, we won't be traumatized by the pain and turmoil of change.

This does not mean that pain isn't real and that surviving a painful experience won't help us mature and grow in our compassion for others. Suffering can be valuable in our life, but it doesn't have to consume or control us. With God's help we can keep it in perspective, learn from it, and let it go.

I am free to interpret whatever pain I may experience today in growth-enhancing ways.

*Once you accept the existence of God—
however you define Him, however you
explain your relationship to Him—then
you are caught forever with His presence
in the center of all things.*

—Morris West

Having our Higher Power as an integral part of how we experience all the hours of a day (whether they hold burdens or blessings) heightens our awareness of the fullness of our life. Believing that God exists for us and in us profoundly changes how we see every aspect of our day. The day and our place in the drama that unfolds take on new meaning and purpose.

A number of us didn't believe in God when we joined a Twelve Step program. Or if we did, many of us believed in a demanding or punishing God who had no relevance to our daily life. What a difference it makes to let a loving God take charge of our thoughts, attitudes, behaviors, and plans for the future. Nothing can stir much fear in us when we remember that God is right here, now, always.

Today God will be the center of all my activities.

*Every happening, great and small, is a
parable whereby God speaks to us, and
the act of life is to get the message.*
> —Malcolm Muggeridge

It's so easy for us to muddle through the day
taking actual notice of very little. We're in conversations we don't really listen to; we read newspaper
articles and novels that we can't recount for
friends; we even sometimes fail to hear another
person's cries for help because we're so self-
absorbed. In all these things, our greatest failing is
that we miss out on God's attempts to get our
attention.

Life is one long adventure in learning—learning
about ourselves, and learning that true joy and
security come from knowing God. No experience is
without purpose in our spiritual unfolding. Our
struggles, our laughter, and our pain can all be
fruitful so long as we are willing to listen to God's
message within each moment. And the real gift is
that we'll release our struggle, the pain will lessen,
and the laughter will deepen.

———————————

*God will reach me today; I will find peace in every
message.*

No one goes his way alone;
All that we send into the lives of others
Comes back into our own.
                              —Edwin Markham

We are not alone—even if we find ourselves temporarily without human companionship. We are part of a fellowship that extends beyond our experience and comprehension. We can take love and sustenance from our own group of special friends. And we can partake of the thoughts and aspirations of our forebears, bridging centuries.

In either place, in our familiar group or in the historical fellowship of humanity, we can give in to loving impulses and satisfy our hunger for spiritual connection. Who has not heard a friend express love or speak a poignant truth and not felt his or her heart moved? It is this access to the best impulses of our fellow creatures, passed down over the centuries or heard just last week, that makes us sure there is a loving force guiding our destiny, inspiring us, and comforting us.

If I feel lonely I can say a prayer, pick up a book, or pick up a telephone, and make a spiritual connection.

*All the good that has ever been or will
ever be has its beginnings in God.*
—Daily Word, *July 11, 1988*

Our inspiration to do small kindnesses for
friends, our desire to express love for those persons
dear in our life, our inclination to offer a smile to a
stranger—all are reminders that God is working in
our life. Our willingness to let God's will be felt by
us and then expressed through us is the most com-
plete contribution each of us can make to this
spirit-filled world that is our home.

However, none of us is yet free from our ego
that, at times, pushes us to act in self-centered,
mean-spirited ways. When we aren't thinking of
God first, we often aren't inclined toward express-
ing our better selves. Fortunately, our program
helps us remember God throughout the day and, in
turn, God gives us opportunities to exercise our
willingness to be kind rather than mean and show
we're thinking of others' needs before our own.

With God's help each of us will share in making
this a better world for all.

---

*I will do my part toward a better world today by
thinking of God during each encounter I have with
another person.*

Relying on God has to begin all over again every day as if nothing had yet been done.

—C. S. Lewis

We often try to turn our will and our life over to the care of God, as we understand God, but we're not always successful. We are human: We change our mind. We talk ourselves out of our good resolutions. We forget. We fall back into old, destructive habits of mind and mood.

But all we have to do is *make a decision*. We don't have to do the actual turning over. We are, in fact, incapable of sustaining this action. But we can, very simply, make the decision. Surprisingly, when we do, turning over our will often gets taken care of for us. We find that we are indeed enjoying what seems to be God's will for us. The secret lies in making the decision as often as needed. We can decide daily or even hourly. We can, in fact, rely on God every time we need help.

This day and every day, I will decide to rely on God all over again.

The more difficulties one has to
encounter, within and without, the more
significant and the higher in inspiration
his life will be.

—Horace Bushnell

Our Higher Power is always with us, through the joyful *and* the fearful times. We often don't remember to think of God though, except when we're troubled. Then our feelings of terror and hopelessness push us to seek help from God, and with this help comes renewed strength and faith that our life is cared for by a greater power than ourselves.

It seems we shouldn't need difficulties to remind us that we can always rely on God, but it's easy to be complacent when times are good. We can choose to expand and strengthen our relationship with God anytime. Through prayer, meditation, and a conscious attempt to feel God's presence in *all* situations, we'll come to know and trust God more fully.

Today I will not wait for a troubling moment to think of God. I'll feel God's presence now!

*Life is what happens to us while we're
making other plans.*
                              —*William Gaddis*

It's easy to let our mind dwell on the future. We may take great pride in being well-organized and able to plan ahead. It's certainly no shortcoming to plan ahead in some instances; many things in life require careful planning. But we can get so focused on planning, that the very life we're given *right now* goes unnoticed.

Each moment is precious, never to return. Whatever we might experience in each moment will not come to us in just that particular way ever again.

We're the losers when we check out on *now* and live in the past or future instead. We can check back in, however, just as quickly as we wandered off. We may need to keep reminding ourselves not to let life pass us by, but with practice, living in the present can become as natural as breathing.

I will remind myself that the moment I'm in is the best part of today.

Anxiety is the natural result when our hopes are centered in anything short of God and his will for us.

—Billy Graham

When we've embarked on a spiritual path, trying to learn the will of God seems essential to our peace of mind. And peace of mind is what we all want.

As we try on a daily basis to improve our conscious contact with God, praying for knowledge of God's will for us, we sometimes find ourselves doing things we never thought we'd do. We may find we're more loving; we treat others as equals; we're more consistently kind, gentle, and considerate. We may begin forgiving others, just as God does us, and find that we catch a glimpse of God in everyone we see. And then we just may discover we are surprisingly free of anxiety.

———————

Today I will seek God's will for me and look for opportunities to express it.

It is the daily strivings that count, not the momentary heights.
—God Calling, January 16

Progress, not perfection, is the hallmark of our program, and spiritual progress is guaranteed when we stay focused on the simple act of loving ourselves and others moment by moment.

Our longing for the one dramatic spiritual experience that will eliminate all uncertainty in our life and guarantee absolute happiness for all time clouds our vision of the moment. And as long as our sights remain on this hoped-for event, we'll continue to miss the spiritual comfort allotted each step of each day's journey.

We need to reflect daily on the progress we've made. Some of us, immobilized by fear in the past, are no longer anxious. Many of us, lonely and isolated in the past, now have caring friends to turn to. And so many of us are now discovering the relief of sincerely asking our God for help.

We grow spiritually even when we seem to be neglecting our spiritual responsibilities. For this we can thank our Higher Power.

———————————

I will open myself with love to each moment today and know that God is close to me each step I take.

Love doesn't just sit there, like a stone; it has to be made, like bread, remade all the time, made new.

—*Ursula K. LeGuin*

Love works through our thoughts, feelings, and actions—it is never static. We are moved as our expressions of love move others. Love soothes, heals, and encourages the fullest expression of who we are meant to be.

God's love is our birthright. We need only open ourselves to this possibility, and we begin to feel the security needed to take the risks each day holds. Just remembering God's love provides strength and ease for today's activities—whether at work or play, we will be less stressful, more joyful.

As we receive God's freely given love, we must give it away and share our courage and strength with others. We pass God's love on each time we share our hope or gratitude or encouragement with a friend. God's love to us and through us will make us whole, will make secure our day.

———————————

My love of others won't be idle today.

*I am not a body. I am free. For I am still
as God created me.*
                    —A Course in Miracles

When we think of ourselves and others as only physical beings, we are limiting our ability to know one another. And we are limiting ourselves. We may be putting too much faith in the looks and condition of our body, thinking that when it fails us, we fail.

We spend great amounts of time planning for the comfort, protection, and enjoyment of our body. Yet we are not just a body. Our natural state is that of a loving spirit.

Our body is outside us, seeming to surround us, keeping us separate from others. But there is no physical barrier between God and us; and the physical barrier between God's sons and daughters is only an illusion—one created by the value we put on our body. When we look at each other, not with our eyes, but with love and forgiveness, the barriers drop and we communicate spirit to spirit.

———————————

Today I will look beyond my body to find a loving spirit.

The manner in which one endures what
must be endured is more important than
the thing that must be endured.
                              —Dean Acheson

Nearly every day most of us experience a few small, though troubling, inconveniences. Some days we suffer through a major setback and, on occasion, even a personal tragedy. When we trust that God is in our life, and we look for comfort and guidance every moment of every day, we are prepared for any upset, whether minor or grave.

Practicing the presence of God provides us with a refuge, even in the throes of turmoil. In time, as we make this a daily routine, we'll seldom doubt God's closeness or feel forsaken, even when all about us is dark. The darkness will give way to the light of hope in the mere moment it takes to remember God's presence.

We can endure whatever lesson today offers with confidence and hope and the security of knowing that God is both teacher and protector.

———————————

I will go through this day confidently in the presence of my Higher Power.

*Success is a process, a quality of mind
and way of being.*
                              —*Alex Noble*

As we think, so we are. And we can use our positive thoughts for successful living by keeping our mind on God's presence in our life, by accepting God's love, and by being willing to trust God's care and direction in our life.

We won't experience failure, doubt our worth, nor question our purpose when we commit our life to the care of God each morning as we prepare for the day. The days will flow more smoothly when God leads us on our journey.

Serenity, joy, and even success can come to us when we let God into our life. Our decisions can be made with confidence when they are directed by God's will.

I will remember God today and find peace and happiness.